A JOURNEY
THROUGH BREATHING

A JOURNEY THROUGH BREATHING

poems

by

jogindra s. siewrattan

Copyright © 2010 by Jogindra S. Siewrattan
ALL RIGHTS RESERVED

The use of any part of this publication, reproduced, transmitted in any form or by any means without the prior consent of the author is an infringement of the copyright law, with the exception of brief passages in reviews.

ISBN: 978-0-9810479-1-1

Edited By: Jogindra S. Siewrattan
Cover Photo: Yale Rosen, M.D.
Layout: Jogindra S. Siewrattan
'About the Author' photo: Pravean Sahadeo

'The Mentally Enslaved' co-written by Truth Is...
'Letters to the Future' co-written by Tomy J. Bewick

Printed & Bound by:
Lulu dot com
North Carolina, USA

Distributed by:
Creative Concepts Graphic & Print
Mississauga, ON Canada

for the ones who have my heart

*we fall and fly
as we climb mountains
descend into chasms*

*our courage
expands and collapses
like lungs*

*every experience
a breath taken*

*without sorrow,
we cannot know laughter
I have fallen and elevated
these words
are my journey*

A Journey Through Breathing

open veined	12
tomorrow	14
my hero	17
walking out of war with flowers on your shoulder (a love poem)	20
red redemption	23
thistle-downs	26
letters to the future	29
lost innocence (broken smiles)	33
victims (soldiers of war)	36
equality	40
coated in rhythm	44
misunderstood	47
affection pt. 2	51
if just for a moment	54
the mentally enslaved	58
my NY mind	62
forever in yesterday	65
feeling like concrete	69
table for two	70
here comes the sun	74

<u>open veined</u>

I bleed frozen moments
I capture them, rapture them
encapsulate them and extract
what I need from them

the sound you hear is not
my voice. it is tales of woes
tales of triumph from lips
of confusion. all of this must
possess some purpose.
some meaning

it comes out of my pores
pours out of my mouth
exhales through the tiny
spaces between my eyes
surrounding my mind's eye

this moment is here
but I am never present
I am gone. looking at now
from the future. through to
the past. at the memory of now
at it happens. transpires
becomes something else

thought is a thief
it steals moments from me
kidnapped from under my nose
for I think and I think and
I think them through

while they may mean nothing
to you. I am constantly trying to
figure out what it means
to me. I bleed moments
for I am cut eternally
they come and they go
I am here and I am not

I transcend the present and
live in the past. thinking about
the future. in this space that
congests with fractures
stacks with journals and
overflows with nows
of yesterday

I am bleeding. have bled
and will continue to bleed
this blood is blue
for it is scattered light that
escapes from me

I am afraid these moments
will escape me forever
so I hold on. I step out. I look in
pull from. keep for
posterity

<u>tomorrow</u>

a dream of tomorrow is in
the wrinkles between my fingers
this world is a test. perpetual. conceptual
you blink the blanket of flesh
smothering your vision of the world
it's like a clean swipe
over the chalk-scripted green board
in the classroom of Officer Pryzbylewski
a fresh start atop residue
of lost knowledge and smudged fingerprints

tomorrow is an illusion
an attainment to aim for through cross-hairs
today is folded paper in sweaty palms
with dirtied corners
secrets once lost. captured into creases of
once untouched canvases

I dream of what the next blink will bring
of how tomorrow will sing
one. two. three. four.
I push. you fall. we cry. we move on.
salt anchors run in straight lines
down the concaves of our cheeks
from the windows of our souls
we fall apart. but we move on

every morning has a meaning of sorts
every breath. until nothing is left
everything remains. as fog in my breath
it dissipates with a push into the atmosphere. disappears

the sun sits on my skin like latex. like shrink wrap

I can see through you
in the moments you see into me
a flash. and I think of places I'd rather be
but like an arsonist I set these places ablaze
because I'd rather be here with you, counting the days
than sailing over seas of troubled water
under smoky skies

it is necessity that tastes like olives on my palette
but in persevering the madness of longing
the settling of these dreams
sits on my tongue sweet like pecan pie

I am always stronger than I want to believe
there are insurmountable feats waiting to be achieved
it's *your* eyes that remind me of this every morning
when I wake up and it's your warmth that I'm adorning

I need to believe. that there's more
to everyday living or I cannot go on
because as hard as the show is. the show must go on
in the moments I feel like I cannot breathe
I hold my breath.
for fear that it might be
the last breath that I have left
for I fear the idea of fear itself
so I tread softly. with caution
as if navigating the intricacies of a shark's mouth
this is where I often find myself. watching myself

hand on shoulder. heart in my mouth

my lungs. hanging from my ears
because I long to hurt. it lets me know that I'm alive
because it's the feeling of feeling itself
that's a reminder of life

I write to survive. to breathe
to find the formula of
every bass beat beneath my breast plate
so I can find tomorrow by figuring out today

a dream of tomorrow is in
the wrinkles between my fingers
when clenched closed they
make way for missed opportunities

so I'd rather live with my hands open
ready to embrace the sun
woven within the tapestry of my palm
welcoming whatever face tomorrow will wear

no matter what I become
I am a culmination of what I was and what I am

I will always count the stars
for this very reason

<u>my hero</u>

I awoke at yesterday's sunrise
with a heavy heart
a wilted sense of purpose. I was tired
but my desire is made of iron
spanning the concave of the earth

the woes of last night's echoes
drifted with time
no hurt can last forever
it's a vehicle of purpose
a window to an expanse of character
that can feel like an insurmountable passing

but this skin
was made to overcome

today. I awoke with
the pulse of potential between my lungs
with brighter eyes than
when I drifted into yester-night's dreams

I do not squint at the sun
I open my pores and close my eyes
to let these moments of enlightenment internalize

I am only destined for my own successes
owning the moments in
the ticking seconds with which God blesses

I do not fly
I do not own tights

but over each hour of every day
across each star scattering the night
I lay myself on the line
in the name of tomorrow

I am a hero
a million little pieces of hope
each one believes in big dreams
every molehill becomes a mountain
holding hands with the sun

I am a dreamer
with my head in the clouds
a carrier of vessels like an ocean
like the wind that knows
it's lending itself to greatness
at the back of an athlete

tomorrow. I will arise
with the sun over my head
a satiated smile
a thousand and one fulfilled dreams
capsized in my eyes

my shoulders will be
as wide as the rings of Saturn
I will have the taste of today's victory
fresh on my tongue

I will pick up despair, trepidation & doubt
I will cradle hate and comfort fear
I will quiet all whispers of opposition
with love and generosity

and the strength of these traits

when they are asleep in my arms
they will awake as flags of triumph. of freedom
as lighthouses on crashing shores

I am a hero
a pioneer of hope
I am all of this
because it is in my blood
in my shoulder blades and knee caps
at the forefront of my mind

but most importantly
it is in my heart
in the belief of belief itself
that overcoming is an understatement
that all of my desires
and moments of realization
live inside of me

walking out of war with flowers on your shoulder
(a love poem)

build me a bridge
grand like the golden gate
string it above water like
taut laces of combat boots
covered in blood

paint it with weather scars
with lashes of thunder
leave the screeching tire marks
of high school sweethearts
leading to busted guardrails
sprinkle the broken glass
painted with their memories
across the asphalt

show me. that pain begets beauty
that regrets are fruitless creatures
that each blade of grass
we look to holds horror stories
tells tales of heroes and loss
epics beginning in sacrifice
the surrender before the ascent

pour me an ocean of smiles
that have been stolen by bad news
like paint thinner splashed on wet walls
the sudden fall of a face
joy surrendered. ~~bled~~. I want to remember
what became of yesterday
by laughter bellowed louder

from remembrance of pain
by retracing footfalls and bloodstains
by your awkward smile and shoe shuffle
when our voices drift in stories
like white noise bleeds in silence
quietly. like whispers on battlefields
that shatter like grand pianos on empty sidewalks

give me shelter.
house me like ashes in an urn
I will decorate your walls with portraits of hearts in return
erect pillars of my missteps
sheetrock plastered with bad decisions
with dead moments hanging from the ceiling
in cracked pots painted with sunshine

I will capture this house.
with all of its wounds
and all of its wonder
into the cupped palm of my hands
to retain the blood so it will not fall
but find itself transformed into rubies

build me a mountain made of corpses
a scrapbook of bodies folded like fingers
standing as tall as my belief in the two of us
my love. my heart
a journal with frayed pages and battered corners
like feet worn ragged on the journey
leading to something wonderful
like eyes blistered from sandstorms
of trying to look into the future

do not show me sunshine from yesterday
this. I will always remember
I need to see where I've been
feel the rain baptize my skin
to count my scars
trace road maps like arteries
up my wrists and over my shoulders

so I can cross these bridges
swim across these oceans made of stolen smiles
and live in a house in a world
that you have gifted me with

I want to light a match in the cavern of your tomb
hear the echo of your heartbeat from inside your womb
cupping palm over flame
finding my heart in your veins

with everything we've created
every future looking back
like light surrounds dust
like darkness rests in sleeping eyes
like you. my love
inside my chest. holding up the walls
when they collapse

red redemption

help me set fire to this apple tree
we'll pluck off all the fruit
place them in perfect pyramids
douse the roots in gasoline
and strike a match to burn it down

for I ate an apple filled with worms
from this very tree
it has lied to me
and I must chop it down
to the size of soiled cat litter

help me set ablaze
the betrayal to my innocence
I will grind its ashes between my teeth
until it flows into my blood stream
so I can make courage from it

burn the branches one by one
chop the trunk up two by two
pluck the leaves off three by three

every piece of the pyramid
is filled with laughing worms
the apples are brown on the inside
green in the middle
and pristinely polished on the outside

it looked so pure
I could not help it
I enjoyed the flavor

it dripped from my chin
but I am rotting from the inside now
just like the flesh of this seedling

all I can do to aim at redemption
is to burn it down
and piss all over the ashes

help me forget my sins
and wash them into the Black Sea
don't ask any questions
just hold the flames with me

pin down the trunk
with hands like needles
we will make it sorry
it ever bore fruit so sweet

grasp the desire to be reborn
scream at the dancing inferno
until your lungs bleed

we will be powerful
when this is all over
we will be inseparable

every time you fall asleep
you will see the dancing tree
turning black and shriveling
withering like frozen fairy tales

we will watch each and every apple
eat itself from the inside out

until the disease devours itself
to find its own cure

this will change our life
this will make us immortal

thistle-downs

silky thistle-downs spin like ballerinas
gaining momentum like a dradle
floating up and sinking down

I can't figure it out

one and one doesn't always equal two
it's invisible cards that trump the
silent, plotting, mathematical types

as much as I resist graph-paper thought
I am a calculator. I am a lens
that shoots only in black and white
only sees straight lines on the road

this waking remnant of thistle
resting at my feet
gusts across black asphalt
to spiral, rise and take flight
spinning and pushing beyond human sight

it serves to remind me of human potential
limitless possibilities and endless roads
there are indecipherable, unpredictable
moments and integers
that will always enter the formula

theorems and components work on paper
in ink. on page. within lines
but off page. I scribble with haste
without pre-determined purpose

for as we assemble each singular value
it is then that we reveal the sum

each piece slowly adds to the whole
when the feathers fill in behind the bones
between shoulder blades
growing fast. geometrically perfected
structured to assemble a flawless arc
flight. and rise in spirit
wingspan outstretch fingertips

it is the things we cannot see
cannot touch or feel. that makes us
more than just men. women. wide-eyed children
creating a biological phenomenon
a gifted progression achieved in earnest desire

giving rise to levitation
excelling beyond our coded potentials
coded categories. formulas. hypotheses
with man-made values and man-made rules

but how can man define these limits
when we cannot see the borders?

we only rest on the sidelines
damning the dreaming by plucking feathers
from the wings of angels

assembling algorithms as
definitive reasoning. when this language
has been spoken for eons. before time even
across galaxies. breaking orbit in silence

past the rims of imagination. into
new telling moments of human potential

when we cast ourselves into the unknown
we can snap our eyelids open
breathing a breath of exponential value
beyond the barrier of sight
to splash black holes into oceans
where there is no bottom
no shore or limit. just simple surface

where we spin like ballerinas. like thistle-downs
skimming the skin of limitless
formless human potential
dreaming of flying
longing for the breeze
to captivate our spirit

while the feathers. and the wings
rest beneath our very own skin
waiting for us to
break the surface

letters to the future

Dear Future,

the prophets have been calling for armageddon
as though the very depths of hell
are not long from this earth's surface
5,000 years ago the Mayans stopped the clock
in the midst of our present
so we hold our breath in anticipation...

Dear Future,

you are not promised. but you are hoped
today knows no tomorrow
like sweet sorrow for the future

I will be in the moon for you
praying we have not doomed you
I poured myself into the sky
put pieces of me in the stars
so I can shine for you
even when I am sleeping

you can find me in the trees
the way roots grip the earth
like an arthritic hand
that will always remember how it came to be
that is me. holding onto a last breath
of every final moment that ever spelt truth
the way leaves dance across
canvases of first loves and last rites

I am in the air that
holds you when you are lost
the one that lifts your chin
and raises your arms
yes. you can fly

we will be your left and right wings
you are something
we never dreamed of beholding
you are an angel
and I dare you to dance with the sun
to forge darkness and light
echo laughter into space

we will live forever in places
you will always feel safe
in earth. in water. in the wind.
eternally we exist within. like fire

beautiful possibility. please believe
you can do more than survive
thrive in the unknown
become freedom in a breath
on mothers' lips of whispered history

Dear Future,

reclaim your mystery
when you fall into the ocean
of abandoned desires
all you need to know is
that you will fall
that you may feel broken

but you will never break

fate ain't got bars big enough for your soul
you may not be promised. but you are our hope
I have condensed every ounce of insecurity
into kilos of determination
to give you as much opportunity to flourish
to nourish your ambition and altruistic ability
we have planted these seeds of seasons to come

that which is to pass shall be a revelation
a panoramic portrait
cast into corners of the unknown
the fear of post apocalyptic
ticking time bombs
of urgent seconds left clicking

Dear Future,

remember me like music
let me fill you with heartfelt lullabies and marching drums
tell you how proud I am to witness your dawn

to watch you rise above the horizon
swallowing the sky. I am reminded
that the future is what we make it
that the spark will continue
to ignite brighter with each passing day
that love will never leave you
even as my memory fades

Dear Future,

the prophets have been calling for armageddon
as though the very depths of hell
are not long from this earth's surface
an ashen existence awaits us
on the precipice of our vision
as we hold our breath waiting...

I will never look away
I need you like a hero
needs something to save
every breath I take fills my lungs
with a purpose that is you
and I will fall into sand
before I ever let you down
if I did I would drown in the ether
a flickering flame without oxygen

you can hear me
when you close your eyes

My Son,
you will be anything your wildest dreams can conceive
there is no such thing as locked doors
because you have all the keys

Dearest Daughter,
this world will be yours through sandstorms and solar rays
remember to hold onto hope. find the silver lining in the grey

I pray you have everything
you need for tomorrow
so I'm working on it
today

lost innocence (broken smiles)

why must children know death?
why must fathers live in fear?
castrated the moment his children are born

helpless at ash strewn across faces
mournful at flies resting on lips
there's no reason for children to exist like this

it's not a foreign face or imported doctrine
it's neighbors. villagers. marketplace kinsmen
PTA constituents. it's brothers and cousins
wrapping themselves in shrouds of cries
for these shrieks give credence
like gasoline to open flames
giving gusto to miscreants

prayers dance across trembling lips
for innocence to be reborn
but bombs put dreams to fitful sleeps
as they grow tall enough to become real

innocence is lost the moment
it opens its eyes to the world
to reveal the ugliness we have painted
with the beauty we have been given

~~~~~~~~~~~~~~~~~~~~~~~

I wipe the blood of children
from the corners of my mouth
stain the tips of my fingers with their cries

yesterday I destroyed twenty-three families
left quaking fathers helplessly trembling
over their dead wives

~~~~~~~~~~~~~~~~~~~~~~

I saw the devil today
he swooped in with talons of an eagle
his eyes were black and he smiled with crooked teeth
the smoke from his gun lifted with
the spray of my son's blood
I lost my reason for living today

~~~~~~~~~~~~~~~~~~~~~~

I write words of condemnation
from the confines of privilege
I waive my finger and
gesture my hands in disapproval
but the truth is…
I've done nothing to change the world

but these words exist for everyone
this hope is for the masses
if action is born of thought
then we have to change our minds
before we can change the world
to listen. to laugh. and let our smiles
emanate our light from within

innocence may be lost
and the future may be in flames
but it burns with potential

it ashens despair.

when we wake up
to shake off the embers
pristine possibilities will be revealed
six billion broken smiles
the innocence of murdered children
that we forget so easily

it's their smiles
that get lost beneath everything
the anger. the hate
the fragmented memories

it's been happening for generations
a disease that cannot be diagnosed
a disease that empowers its victims
and crushes the innocent

it's the sound of laughter
that evaporates into
strings of forgetful smoke
lifting from lives burning
in wake of someone else's triumph

victims (soldiers of war)

they say they're tired of hearing stories
about American soldiers
stories that highlight the plight
of Americans and their suffering
the sad, little lives
of gun-toting Americans
who kill innocent people every day

that it's about time
they heard the story of
a real victim of war
someone who has really suffered loss

but who is a real victim of war?
what do they look like?
there are casualties that we
cannot see or ever understand
casualties that die inside
while the living keep on living
but those are dead men walking

they sit in living rooms
with power to condemn
and rub the names of
countless dead soldiers
into the ground because
they only see a flag

they only see two countries
the rhetoric between them
but if you take away the American flag

take away the politics
strip away the soldier's uniform
then what do you have?

you have a human being
a tightly wound thing that lives
and breathes and trembles in fear
a bundle of nerves hanging on razor blades

you have a husband and a father
a young boy hoping
to carve the word *meaning*
into the tree of life

a stone cold killer
with ice in his eyes
who melts into his sheets every night

a man forsaken by his country
left to fend for himself
because they protest the war at home
but they forget about him
trying to survive
where he is not wanted

he may or may not believe
in the fight he is fighting
but brothers in arms are brothers in blood
a brotherhood we can never understand

and they sit there
on thrones of complacency
in kingdoms of doubt

and belittle the emotional depth
of a solider and his family
because of the flag that he flies

I thought we could at least pretend
to understand how it must feel
to open the door and see 2 men
standing on your *welcome* mat
telling you your life is over
and you never got to say goodbye
now you get to cradle a picture to sleep

that we could empathize with
sons and daughters losing their role models
with what it takes to write a last letter
every time you suit up to face the bullets

that has nothing
to do with political policies
or rhetoric or presidencies
or any label that can be placed on it
that has to do with humanity

in war. nobody wins
every side loses something
they can never get back

every victim has a voice
that has nothing to do
with stars or stripes
or maple leafs
or crescent moons and stars

that voice has to do with the sun
it has to do with loss
things that cannot be touched
but can easily be killed
it has to do with innocence
with last rites and second chances

it has to do with people
not flags.
anything. but flags

<u>equality</u>

some people say they want equality
but all they see is color
they write about peace
while they only talk about war
they cry of injustice
and dry their eyes on discrimination

these double-edged dagger tongues
are cutting their mouths
every time they speak
they are spewing blood
like open wounds

they'll never see
that things will never change
as long as the system
has them wearing these glasses
every time they speak
I can hear the swine laughing

full-bellied bellowing
at their indifferent ignorance
instead of treating people with compassion
they insist on placing borders around smiles
they are determined to limit a heart's potential

but we are all one consciousness
so how could anyone pioneer justice
with hatred and decrees of war?
try to listen to the leaders
who set nations free

the leaders who actually fought mental slavery

Mohandas Karamchand Ghandi. never raised a fist
Martin Luther King Junior. never raised a fist

yet somehow. we find words like
freedom. independence. liberation
encased in asterisks beside their names

meanwhile. you have so-called revolutionaries
pumping their blood-soaked fists for causes
while they only know half-truths
if you live your life by statistics
you're bound to become a number
they can't see that lines don't exist
that's why they keep drawing them in the sand

maybe I can't understand
because of who I am
the branches of my family tree
have so many roots
my mother's lineage
traces back to the Arawak Natives
across the Atlantic Ocean to Spain
a Boriqua birthed in Manhattan
my great grand father migrated
from India to cut sugar cane
so my father. was born in the
land of calypso. Trinidad & Tobago
he passed through a Jack Kerouac tale
of smoggy American cities

for me to be born in Baton Rouge, LA

then I moved to Fort Lauderdale
of every culture underneath the sun
I was learning that
I was never a single one

but I've also learned
none of that matters
I choose to share this space
with the faces that God's created
so I have brothers of so many races
sisters from so many places

the world will always be my family
I can only offer my hand to my enemy

so excuse me.
if I don't see color the way they insist to
excuse me
if I can't stand up and pump my fist for my people
it's only because I have so many of them
excuse me
if I can't excuse them because I can be color blind
and they cannot

when they talk in bigoted phrases
against the very ideas
that are planted like seeds upon their tongues
it makes me see them as nothing but fools
as broken-backed mules
carrying intentions they cannot see

they talk of freedom
they talk of liberation

they talk a real big talk.

but they are blind-folded
wading naked through a forest of thorns
drawing blood from the future before it becomes
this is the legacy that's left behind
what's being taught to generations to come
they're putting hate in the minds of the little ones

I wish I could open their eyes before it's too late
we only have today to create tomorrow
but they keep tightening the noose on the future
fabricating truth from a factory of lies

God help us all
they have become slaves
to everything they despise

<u>coated in rhythm</u>

I love my poet friends
they paint immaculate murals
from mundane monotonous moments

my everyday friends
incessantly talk about work

I don't even know where half
my poet friends work. they never say
we'd rather know our alter-egos
those super-hero poets
who can slay nay-sayers with their tongues

I love my poet friends
we talk about things we cannot touch
things that make the hair on our skin stand
things we can reach with our voices

they'd rather eat metaphors for main courses
and similes for course-capping dessert dishes
words coated in rhythm and juxtapose
they smell the roses
they see the beauty in everything

they also see every grim detail
every worst-case-scenario
every lingering doubt in a dream

because that is the way of imagining
so sometimes I loathe us poets
I loathe even being one

sometimes I would rather
just to see the surface of things
and not be prone to seeing
molding in cracks
of statuettes that are beautiful
sometimes I would rather bathe
in the bliss of ignorance

but then I would be lost
without words like nuance and cadence
and rhythm and supple
without metaphor I would not be myself
so I surround myself with poets
as I surround myself with poetry
and drown myself in poems

most of all though…I miss my poets
my wordsmiths from across provinces
state-lines and open oceans
I miss my people from Florida
the ones from California. VanCity represent
Chicago. Green Mill. Writing Wrongs
Black Pearl. Njozi Poets
Every face from the
National Poetry Slam 2008 in Madison, WI
Oberlin. Capital City. Honolulu Slam
Markham. Burlington. London
New York City. Orlando and North Carolina
the cities that I never knew
because we got lost in verse
so logistics were never dispersed

I miss their voices over breakfast
over chips and chatter in pubs
but I miss their faces even more
all of you give me a reason to keep writing
a reason to want to be a better person

when I hear your elaborate symphonies
my ears are grateful to exist in those moments
everything ceases to exist in those sentences
I wind up finding myself within those stanzas

if we could live half of the things
that we create with our words
we would be immaculate creatures
and you keep pushing me into greatness

I could spew endlessly
about how much you and
your verses mean to me
but the simplest of sentiments
speaks the most direct to me

I love my friends. every day
especially, when they are
coated in rhythm

misunderstood

lately. I feel like a shadow
trailing towers that wish I wasn't there
like a can of tear gas
plucked and Hail Mary'ed
into a crowd of co-workers
rioting against my difference of opinion

I wonder what brings about
the unrest that rests in their hearts
their sad, little hearts
trying to figure me out
devising formulas to find my thought patterns

but they will never know my numbers
their formulas will never add up
there are too many variables
like which 'me' comes into work
which grade of will walks through the door

I am introverted by choice
withdrawn like unsolicited death threats
uttered from peacemakers to warlords

I am a thousand opportunities
waiting to happen
like petals of a lotus flower the size
of New Orleans' Superdome
unfolding and falling
like the ashes of the Twin Towers
smothering passer-bys in my memories
and they are left wondering

where the falling sentiments came from

you can bask me in the innocence
you no longer possess
cover me in your guilt
douse me in the flames
in which your house is burning
I will take the abuse
the fire will not burn me

I will flip two coins and call for a truce
I will call for fifty-fifty twice in a row
so that we can both win

I call for myself to step to the plate
grip with two hands
and swing away. swing away. swing away
you will perish the moment I burst free
anyone who tried to bring me down
to chop me into pieces
you will rest in the dead skin
across my finger tips

I call for you to believe in me
and save yourself from me
because the moment I turn this thing on
you're going to die a terrible death
you're going to be incinerated
I can smell it

I'm beginning to know it's in my knuckles
so anyone who ever laughed at my dreams
you kept me on the lower rung of the ladder

for your own self-worth
get ready to fall 1,000 stories
I will watch you shatter on the ground

I cannot let you tear me down anymore
I will not let you have me believe I am less
I will not believe I am more in the same breath
I will not adopt your beliefs

I still believe you can be a better person
that is the difference between us
I am not a destroyer
I do not admonish the existence of beauty
but if you must die. then so you will
your memory will be the scathe of my history
the bitter side of me will tuck you into nothingness
grind you under my teeth like chewing tobacco

for it is you who seeks salvation
banging on pots to scare away your demons
but they are in your ribcage
they are in your very eyes
so you cannot see them

you can only taste them like the disdain
you hold in contempt
and smell them like the sulfur
of burnt out matches

I am tired of living like this
so to you I will say good-bye
if you need me. then
you know where to find me

but if you speak in the tongues
from which you've always existed
then you are dead to me

I no longer need you to breathe
you will be a memory
still trying to understand me
long after the
ashes have been scattered

affection pt. 2

he spews pixie dust from the tips of his lips
it captivates desire like a star can capture a wish
springs forth fairy tales meant to capture you
words dripping with flatteries meant to rapture you
Peter Pan. Neverland. Princess Brides
fabler. enabler. purveyor of lies

he speaks in riddles. in fables
his words are like stilts. like gables
his smile is a one-sided grin
like a half-cocked pistol
pretty and prickly like full-bloomed thistle
with eyes that look into every one of her souls
every little skirt plays the same role

they're all the same
the lost, teary-eyed girl
the can-do, powerful woman
even the dreamer. longing to believe
lost in thoughts she cannot conceive
it's easy to see what they think they need
if you open your ears you can hear their pleas
she wants to feel loved
catered for. taken care of

he can be the father she never had
he can wear the hat of dear ole dad
no matter how many faces he must wear
he is determined to get her to where
she will trust him with her life
no matter the cost or the price

he knows these situations all too well
so he always ended up with a story to tell
occupied fathers. breed unfulfilled daughters
unfulfilled becomes unwanted
becomes ugly. becomes untouchable. unlovable
and spirals like a top
around and around
until some one falls down

he towers over with extended palm
all the while singing sad love songs
for words are just what she needs
to allow him to do his evil deeds

but he is only getting what he wants
while tying her in water knots
using her like a car. but she's the one driving
breaking red lights just barely surviving
she changes gears at his whim
hits the gas and turns the wheel for him
she stops for him. but never runs from him
even when his hand raises in anger
when he berates her like a stranger

when his beautiful words
shift to ugly. change to hate
the prince of thieves becomes irate
a diatribe of insults spews from the tips of lips
a betrayal to every once gentle kiss
aimed at any feeling of self-worth
and like a card to a clock. it works

he says his positives outweigh his negatives
that he doesn't mean any of his expletives
that she deserves everything she receives
all of the markings that he leaves
the bruised hip. the twisted wrist
the broken heart. the busted lip

she's no longer even good for sex
because she shivers in his presence
quivers at his once tender touch
the one she used to love so much

when he is finished he will
wash his hands of her and walk away
there will be nothing left for him to say
onto the next lost, teary-eyed girl
the can-do, powerful woman
the dreamer. longing to believe
lost in thoughts she cannot conceive
because it's easy to see what they think they need
if you open your ears you can hear their pleas

but the truth is…he needs their weak hearts
more than he can realize
that is why he dresses in his disguise
for he cannot exist without
the tortured love of these tortured souls
without them he would be
less than half of a whole
a sheep amidst wolves. a boy amongst men
he would be powerless without his dear women

if just for a moment

for Neeka

I remember you through stages
moments that stand still for me

being proud of myself
for the first flashes in my life
feeling like I had a purpose
I owe that to you

you have to understand your Uncle
I need a reason for everything. even if it's to breathe
and you gave me that purpose
even if it was just for a moment

I remember laughing with you
on Sunday mornings over bowls of cereal
about nothing. about everything

I remember chasing you around the house
arm stretched out like trees
taking you swimming
you crafted an ocean in our backyard
it came like nothing. but means so many things

I searched for ways
to comb your hair without making you cry
because it broke my heart

we found that way after a while
you were content and calm every time

even if it was just for a moment

if I could peel back time for posterity
I would keep the second year of your life
in the chest pocket of every shirt
I would stitch the memories to my fingertips
because you made me who I am
even if it was just for a moment

my moments of confidence
my moments of desperation
the times I was ready to scream
... then you would smile
and we would laugh again

I was so afraid of you growing up
I kept my distance for years
peeking at you from around corners
now you're a young lady
taking broad steps into life
jumping head first. arms out
into everything you can

I wish I could show you the world
show you that it's all yours
in every form and fashion you can fathom
but that it's not going anywhere
it will always be waiting for you

take your time.
when you drive so fast
you miss everything worth seeing
the landmarks. the lessons

you can't see the details in blurs
brushed at the side of your vision

I wish I could give you wings to grow
show you that you can fly
and that when you fall
you must stand up on your own
this is the joy of learning
the way your heart beats
listen to the rhythm
if just for a moment

don't grow up too fast
believe me. I know
you will miss these years
when they are gone
because time is not
something you can get back
before you know it…it's gone

laugh without borders
go roller-skating. have sleep-overs
play basketball. run as fast as you can
until you feel your heart speak to you
from beneath flesh. and ribs
thanking you for the adrenaline
every stage was meant to run its course
to be cherished like treasure

I remember you through stages
moments that stood still for me
the first night I carried you
from the car-seat to your crib

without waking you
you slumbered on my shoulder
I watched you sleep for a moment
it was absolutely amazing

you're a young woman now
running through forests of trees
shedding skin. losing yourself
leaving behind all that was
to find the woman you will become

I see you growing like ripples in a pond
like petals of a budding flower
but don't open too quickly
shed your skin slowly
hold onto the way it feels
even if it's just for a moment
you will miss it
when it's gone

<u>the mentally enslaved</u>

when people
forcefully occupy space
self-assigned to others
holding different beliefs
they become invaders

the effects are many and long withstanding

in the modern Indian film industry
dark brown skin is a scarcity
it's not that it doesn't exist
it just doesn't represent what
the mentally enslaved consider beautiful

for modern African descendants. it's hair
through cycles and systems and slavery
they now believe their hair is substandard

the religion of their ancestors is lost because
generations of Christianity & Islam
have blanketed these ideas as savage

what was once sacred falls like
a king toppling over on broken legs
the prince plunges into pines of piety
pawns pace in a race to become queens
of a hastily assembled government body
or an elaborate system of oppression

whatever you call it,

the mechanism is violent
forsaking smiling times for smirks of war
leaving the newly appropriated soil of our minds scarred
forced to absorb the blood of its many children

you. are beautiful

no pawn is safe from the murderous knights
villages are pillaged. women are raped
poets have their throats slit
in the town's checkered square
for choosing blood before silence

although sometimes. the insurgence is peaceful
they come in the form of conversion
carved into the upturned palms
of missionaries and bishops chanting
we will save you
*but you must pray to **our** God*

if only it were a small price to pay for salvation
all this to create a legacy
one that will not look like our children

when the kingdom eventually collapses
know that it will never be a matter of defeat
just the belly of the beast has been appeased

so we rest our guards, believing we are free again
but are left with the idea that our belief system is flawed
the castle has fallen, but the rooks remain
like security poised over our image

and suddenly, the people assigned
to the self-possessed space
who were once free. who were once occupied
are not free at all, but mentally enslaved

look back, look around
you will notice that the countries richest in culture
still remain steeped in the seed of their conquerors

but the culture crafted by a people is resilient
and like a whisper of a howl in the cold of night
there is a resurgence occurring
as people mix and people mingle
we are beginning to realize
that behind curtains painted in illusion
there are beautiful Indian women
with dark, brown skin

there are Africans still practicing the religion
of their ancestors from before Christ
there are modern African descendants
who wear their hair natural

when the world calls you beautiful
you have to consider that you are
when it calls you ugly
you have to consider that they are blind

people around the world have
a culture that was always their own
it is longing to be embraced
but first it has to be found

the mentally enslaved are roaming like nomads
but slaves...were always meant to freed

my NY mind

it's still the way it began
so many generations ago
a thousand opportunities
etched in the eyes of the eager
grimaced beneath a Yankee fitted
underneath the skin of the streets
the heartbeat still rhymes the same way
still rhythms to the same sway
as way back then

after the birth of so many great people
it's still. the city of promise
where anything's possible
any path holds a thousand futures
the I-95. GWB. upstate I-90. Hudson River. Ellis Island
Lincoln Tunnel. LaGuardia. Brooklyn Bridge
a twisted cacophony of flashing lights
a star in the sky to throw wishes at
like pennies in puddles of water
it sparkles. like the North Star on a wandering night

it's violently beautiful
irresistibly desirable
grotesquely admirable
so big it blows your mind
the city of guns. the land of love
quick to swallow a little man's big dreams
the law of the land
like bigger fish eating little ones
the city that never sleeps. always awake
statue of liberty. the empire state

that's where I am sometimes
the half side of my country-filled youth
a world I can only be drawn to naturally

the city called to my Pops when he was 25
brought him to the Boogie Down
boiling hot 70's melting pot
met my Mom and fell in lustful love
it was undeniable
the Bronx brought Puerto Rico and Trinidad
together like the subway and the city

my Mom was made in Manhattan
my Brother lives in Queens
Uncle over in Yonkers. now upstate
Grandma. still in the building
on Father Zseizer Place
across the street from the park
where I got my first Sega Genesis stolen
Fordham & University. back in 80-something
The Bronx.

the streets were alive
the people were ugly
but damn! they were beautiful
animating local languages beyond linguistics
they were anything I was not
I hid behind my Dad's jeans
afraid of the breathing monster
surrounding my terrified little heart
clutching close to the car
afraid of becoming lost in the hustle

beautiful concrete jungle

Times Square at any time of any day
you stand a divided continent
one foot basking in greatness
the other drenched in obscurity
eyes over and above the building-tops
the skyline eats me alive
and I offer myself gladly
because I want to be the city
I want to feel it like the sun

New York City.
the city of dreams
of abandoned children
sought after men and women
palace of lost loves
refuge for forgotten ones
it can be anything you'd ever dream of
a beast. a beauty. a beacon
whatever it is. it's the same as it always was
and always will be
a shooting star for the awe of daydreamers
heartbreakers. romancers. song-singers. break-dancers
wall-streeters. story-weavers
risk-takers. life-takers. deal-breakers
poets. perverts. politicians. addicts & thieves
nobody's. somebody's. and everybody's home
this beautiful, monstrous metropolis

<u>forever in yesterday</u>

I want my mother back
I miss the woman who
smiled with every other heartbeat
life was tough. dealings were bitter
in flashing pictographs
of fragmented yesteryears

life is a collection of stories
a grand painting of tiny moments
where laughter wasn't the best medicine
it was our way of existing

I miss my Mom
I haven't seen her in four years
it's not the sound of her voice that I miss
it's the mother I remember
the *dust yourself off and step back in* Mom

there are times I forego a phone call
so I don't have to hear her complain
about how hard life is
about how there's no way out

one thing she taught us
was when lights go out
when only darkness can be seen
trains fly off tracks in flips and furies
bending metal and shattering hope
into tiny shimmers of smiles
like snips of hair on kitchen floors

but what was once broken
battered beyond recognition
yearns to be reborn into stronger skin
a stronger sense of purpose

where can I find these lessons?
where is the woman who was happy to be alive?
was able to overcome adversaries unthinkable
to today's quick-to-quit society

I know she must be tired
it hasn't gotten easier
not by one grain of sand
or one strand of hair

it's the bitterness I don't understand
smiling through clenched teeth
I feel like a an ungrateful spoiled child
for feeling this way
like an unrealistic son

but you have to understand
if Atlas was a woman
then it was my world she lifted
it was my mother
under the weight of the planet
she would never crumble
her knees stood like the legs of the Eifel Tower
she was unbreakable

so when I answer the phone

to ask her how she is. it's bittersweet
because I'm forced to let go of childhood
every time. look at her at eye level
see the weight of the years

I look for her lessons everywhere
I pick them up like carefully crafted Easter eggs
I find omens like Matthew Perry did in *Fools Rush In*
my mother's favorite movie

these are the places I find the wonderment
left in the remains of her storybook endings
I wish I could tell her it would be okay
and have her believe me
if only I could have her believe in Stone Soup
but I'm left speechless every time
I come to understand my heroes' villains

I sit at the other end of the line
waiting for the woman that raised me to come out
she is so strong she can move mountains
I never know what to say to the person
who taught me of greener pastures
of silver linings and colorless emotions
of dancing to Julio Iglesias while cleaning the house

I miss my mother
I want to help her find her way back
to her body of work. to her.
tucked in a forest of charcoal-etched trees
she created across this canvas
if I had the courage I would say:

*I'm collecting these eggs for you Mother
whenever you fall apart. whenever you slip away
you leave me a crumb
and I will find you through this
I will find you the most beautiful of stories
a masterpiece of life
an orchestra of bedtime stories*

*this basket of crumbs. and eggs. and stones
is everything you have given me over the years
and now I'm giving it back*

<u>feeling like concrete</u>

I hang my head when I feel like this. *defeated*
like something inside is gone for good. *depleted*
I walk with my shoulders draped in. *withdrawn*
feeling with remembrance what I wish I was. *strong*
trying to convince myself what I must be. *wrong*

I walk as close as I can to the walls. *attached*
looking for foundation instead of feeling. *detached*
I step over cracked concrete. *broken ground*
so I can feel that my footing is solid. *sound*
but a loss is a loss and I remain defeated. *behind*
as my yards of self-worth becomes undone. *unwind*

I tuck my hands into my pockets up to my. *knuckles*
my steps, one by one get lower. *buckles*
as far as I've come, it's still easy to feel like this. *small*
and I pray for stilts to stand on to make me feel. *tall*

<u>table for two</u>

crack me like uneven concrete
I am divided as the souls of Kashmir

sometimes life gives you pictures
you cannot see with your eyes
these pictures are not meant
to hang on walls
they are meant to show you
who you can become
if you only listen
to the whispers behind the rain
for once. stop trying
to side-step the inevitable
stop trying to dodge raindrops
you were meant to be drenched

these are moments where
you peel away layers of skin
plunge your fingers deep
into veins behind your sternum

that is where these pictures go
you hang them on the inside of your ribs
for we can never understand them
with our eyes. only with our hearts

until this image finds clarity
until I find a reason for this
I am worn as thin as a widow's vale
one that cannot hide tears
one that cannot paint a face for me

I am clear, concise
and obviously drowning

sometimes you have to
wear the face of an emperor
you have to be ever-noble
not contentious. but always graceful
you have to hold your desire
to destroy everything in sight

when everything you thought you knew
proves unreliable. more malleable
than you can ever conceive

the only thing that will bring you down
from this rollercoaster of humility
is losing your humanity
in front of the ones you love most
the ones who love you dearly
you want to scare them into retreating steps
and shatter any picturesque setting
that feels like it's lying to you

but you cannot. you must fight this
like addiction. like unwanted love
you must consider your place in the universe
your place in time. it is miniscule
and you must leave behind
some strength to be remembered by

sometimes the world is bigger
than you can ever be

I am in a thousand places
at this very instant
so count me like passing cars
like prayers rolled over rosary beads
how many *me's* will it take
to conquer my demons?

even as I swallow this reality
there is a *me* inside screaming
wanting to break out of his cage
rattle everyone like earthquakes
and tell them they're all out of their minds

that is my Monster
he must exist for me
to think the way I do
his solution is always savage

sometimes I become him
in my mind
but almost never in this world
I choose to remain divided in two
for I am afraid of aftermath
of what he is capable of
so I speak to myself out loud
in reassuring parables

I am a babbling buffoon
who makes sense to no one
not even myself
a wandering vagrant
begging for grains of salt

but when I open my mouth
I speak in tongues
they do not understand the tormented
writhing in front of their eyes
all in my face

I want to be heard like a symphony
but someone has stolen
my violin and cello strings
they've made away with
all of my brass mouth pieces
reeds and drumsticks
so I am a soundless symphony

I am voiceless
a punctured lung trying to breathe

my own worst enemy
cutting my veins open
just to see how I bleed

<u>here comes the sun</u>

I blink in thunder claps
it rumbles when my eyes close
the clashes of my lashes spring forth lightning
rattling the insides of my cornea
with sideways, stinging rain
I am engulfed in a world of possibilities
raining on me like unforgiving heartache
like free-falls of laughter

when I am cold
I nestle into corners that feel like home
corners of abandoned desires
of warmth on windy afternoons
these desires. they hold me in promise

I'm going to pass this on it seems
because every time I touch my wife's stomach
he nestles into a corner. a one-sided womb
tilted like a burlap sack of unknown fruits

I want this to mean something
I want everything to mean everything
and I want nothing to stay in its house
lock the doors and close the shades
I don't want to see her anymore (this nothing)
I'm building a new house
right atop my old one

I've got stilts stretching from the roof
like a garden of wind turbines. with one chimney
no smoke. just ashes

pristinely clean window panes. crystal clear glasses
no guilt in the closet. no shame on the mirrors

I've installed garbage disposals in every room
so when these feelings come back
I can accordion crumple them in and flip the switch
I've even made the floor out of glass
so I can see my steps long after I've made them
foggy residues of oil telling my story
with the old *me* gazing up
to see what we'll become

I left out all doors
I never want them closed
I want to be open all the time
so I can never lose myself
behind locked latches of wondering
what's waiting for me on the other side

I want to leave diamonds everywhere I fall
diamonds the size of dust
I've got months to go
and I'm still trying to believe
to do the right thing
to create more white blood cells
I know I am going to make it

I've been doing some heavy lifting
sawing the rope painstakingly slow
cutting anchors into flat-lined oceans
so I can leave this all behind
and sail into a new horizon

his little smile makes me believe
that I have made it already
her eyes let me know that I'm okay
when I hold the two of them
in the warmest parts of my heart
I don't blink in thunder claps anymore

I blink in rising suns
in new days warm enough to harbor desires
so I can find them waiting for me
in days warm enough for my dreams
to grow into living things with wings

it is on these days
that I count my blessings in the morning
say my prayers in the evening

the journey was worth every step
every drop of rain
flash of lightning

the destination *is* everything
but it is nothing without thunder
and rain. and those corners
that feel like home

Acknowledgments:

I would like to take a moment and acknowledge a few of the inspirations and co-conspirators in my work:

'The Mentally Enslaved' was a work in progress for a very long time until Truth Is... helped me find the poetry in the facts, thank you.

Jay-Z's 'Empire State of Mind' made me remember how much I love NY and inspired me to write 'My NY Mind'

I would like to thank Yale Rosen, M.D. for granting me permission to use his image. It perfectly illustrates what I wanted to capture within this book.

about the image:
In the very center is a terminal airway (terminal bronchiole) that conducts inspired air into the lungs. Surrounding this structure are the air spaces (alveoli) and the thin alveolar walls that appear to radiate outward from the central airway. These air spaces contain air. The alveolar walls contain small blood vessels (capillaries). Oxygen from the inspired air in the alveoli diffuses into the capillaries and then circulates to the entire body. Carbon dioxide, a "waste product' of the body's metabolism diffuses out of the capillaries and into the alveoli and exits the body when a person exhales. At the bottom of the image in the left lower quadrant there is a small pulmonary artery containing red blood cells

about the author:

Jogindra Siewrattan was born in Baton Rouge, Louisiana. He now lives with his wife, son and daughter in Mississauga, Ontario.

He has performed at spoken word and reading series across the Greater Toronto Area such as The Art Bar Poetry Series, Cryptic Chatter, Strong Words, CBC Poetry Face-Off 2009, Luminato Poetry Slam 2008 & When Words Are Spoken. He has taken part in Eden Mill Writer's Festival 2008 National Poetry Slam 2008, QEW Regional Slams 2009, 2010 & 2011 and The Canadian Festival of Spoken Word 2010 & 2011..

Yogi is also an artist who has worked with Quattro Books, Burning Effigy Press, The Brampton Neighborhood Resource Centre, The Roots Lounge Poetry Slam and Toronto Poetry Slam. He has worked on spoken word albums for artists Leviathan, Soulfistikato and Tomy Bewick.

ॐ

www.ingramcontent.com/pod-product-compliance
Ingram Content Group UK Ltd.
Pitfield, Milton Keynes, MK11 3LW, UK
UKHW041958230426
12048UKWH00008B/411